B **Global Warming and the Arctic.** R
each word or phrase with the correct def

Polar bears live on the ice pack of th
the ice for their food and survival since it is a primary hunting ground
for seals and beluga whales. However, due to global warming, the Arctic
ice is thawing earlier and freezing later every year. This means the polar
bears that live in Canada's Hudson Bay area must wait longer for the
ice—and the food that comes with it—to arrive. This situation has
become a great threat to the entire species.

1. ice pack _____	**a.** a large body of water partly surrounded by land
2. seal _____	**b.** a small, dark animal with flippers that lives in cold waters
3. beluga whale _____	**c.** a huge, warm-blooded animal shaped like a fish and found in the ocean
4. global warming _____	**d.** the slow turning of ice into water
5. thaw _____	**e.** a specific group of living things that have similar characteristics
6. bay _____	**f.** a large area of ice that floats on the ocean
7. species _____	**g.** an increase in world temperatures caused by gases that stop heat from escaping into space

polar bear

An Arctic Ice Scene

Near the edge of the Arctic region of Canada, the short summer is rapidly disappearing. The sun is pale, and the brief days of fall are being chased away by a constant cold wind from the north. Along the western shore of the Hudson Bay, winter is beginning to close its grip and make this a very **inhospitable**[1] environment. It's an icy cold region in which few animals or plants can survive.

One animal, though, actually **thrives**[2] in these freezing, lonely surroundings: the polar bear. Every year on the western edge of the Hudson Bay, polar bears hungrily wait for the freezing of the bay in order to begin their hunting season. Winter has the perfect weather for this huge white bear, which is the world's largest land carnivore and an animal that depends on the ice and cold for its survival. What is it about this remarkable and beautiful marine mammal that makes it particularly suited for such extreme temperatures?

---

[1] **inhospitable:** not welcoming; unfriendly
[2] **thrive:** grow strong and healthy

🎧 CD 1, Track 03

Skim for Gist

Read through the entire book quickly to answer the questions.

1. What is the main message of the book?

2. What are the main reasons that the polar bear is at risk?

According to Cam Elliot of the governmental group called 'Manitoba Conservation,' "Polar bears are built for winter. They're built for the cold." He then continues, "They're built for the wind." These warm-blooded mammals spend most of their lives on frozen seas, so they have adjusted to be able to handle the cold weather. The animals' thick fur protects and **insulates**[3] them from the freezing winds. Polar bears also have short tails and small ears, both of which help to reduce heat loss. In addition, they are able to keep reserves of blubber on their bodies. This aspect of their development has helped them to survive the Arctic in two ways. The heavy layer of fat helps to protect the animals from the cold, and it also allows them to live for long periods of time without eating.

Polar bears depend on the frozen ice packs covering large bodies of water in order to hunt and get their food. Unfortunately, polar bears along the western shore of the bay don't enjoy the luxury of an uninterrupted winter. Elliot explains that the ice is not permanent in the area, which is why polar bears in this region are often seen on the land during the summer. "With the **onset**[4] of summer and the warmer temperatures, all of Hudson Bay melts," he points out before adding, "Unlike the high Arctic, there's no permanent ice pack here. When the bay melts, the bears are forced to [go to] shore."

---

[3]**insulate:** protect; keep warm
[4]**onset:** the beginning of something

It is a seasonal life for the bears in this region. When the weather starts to turn cold again, large numbers of them gather around the coast of the bay, and can be seen along the shore. At this time, these typically private animals will interact in ways not completely understood by humans. They play or fight with each other, all the while waiting for the bay to freeze completely so that they can go back to the ice and their food source. Until that happens, the bears are **stranded**[5] on the shore, unable to go anywhere. It is at this time that polar bears and human beings have a chance to safely come into contact.

As the bears wait for the coming of the ice, people begin to arrive from nearby towns and cities. They drive across the wide, open land surrounding the bay in strange-looking vehicles. These 'tundra buggies' are special truck-like vehicles that are designed for rough travel. By riding in them out to the shore, people can take advantage of a wonderful opportunity. They can get a chance to observe these rare and fascinating animals, which can very rarely be seen outside of films or zoos, in their natural environment. Here, they are able to use **binoculars**[6] to view the polar bears quite closely and observe their behavior, both alone and with other bears.

---

[5]**stranded:** be left somewhere with no way of returning
[6]**binoculars:** glasses that make distant objects seem closer and larger

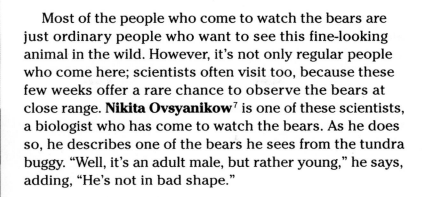

Most of the people who come to watch the bears are just ordinary people who want to see this fine-looking animal in the wild. However, it's not only regular people who come here; scientists often visit too, because these few weeks offer a rare chance to observe the bears at close range. **Nikita Ovsyanikow**[7] is one of these scientists, a biologist who has come to watch the bears. As he does so, he describes one of the bears he sees from the tundra buggy. "Well, it's an adult male, but rather young," he says, adding, "He's not in bad shape."

No other animal hunts the polar bear; they are at the top of the **food chain**.[8] Because of their status as 'top killers,' scientists feel that polar bears can be considered relatively good indicators of the health of the Arctic environment. Ovsyanikow explains, "What is especially attractive in polar bears in terms of conservation, [is that] it is [an] **umbrella species**.[9] It's a large predator which is [at] the top of the food chain in the Arctic." This means that biologists such as Ovsyanikow can tell a lot about the condition of the Arctic environment by studying the polar bear. It also means that the health of the polar bear species reflects the health of a number of other species in the Arctic region.

---

[7] **Nikita Ovsyanikow:** [nɪk̠itə ɔfsyɑnɪkɔf]
[8] **food chain:** a scientific term for a series of living things in which one group eats another
[9] **umbrella species:** a species which can be considered representative of the animal life in a particular area

As the people and scientists watch the bears, the animals can be observed desperately trying to find something to eat in the frozen earth—they even try to eat grass. "They're hungry," observes polar bear guide **John Bykerk**.[10] At this time of year, the built-up fat reserves that have kept the polar bears alive since the ice melted, have served their purpose. Sadly, the bears' bodies are starving for energy by now, and some are beginning to look thin. It's not surprising that the bears are hungry; it's been a long time since they've eaten anything at all. Bykerk explains, "Unless they're lucky enough to find some dead beluga whale or some dead seal, perhaps that's washed up on shore, they've essentially gone four months at this point without having a bite to eat."

---

[10]**John Bykerk:** [dʒɒn baɪkɜrk]

Many researchers believe that the health of polar bears parallels directly with the health of the environment. Scientists are concerned that despite the constant cold in Northern Manitoba, it may not be staying cold long enough to keep the environment stable. In other words, global warming may be affecting the ice patterns, which are critical for the survival of the polar bear.

Cam Elliot explains what the situation means for the continued existence of the polar bear. "Over the last twenty-five years, research conducted by the Canadian Wildlife Service has found about a two-week advancement in spring weather and ice melt," he reports. "Polar bears are a creature of the sea ice. When they're out on the ice, they're hunting seals. Anything in the global climate that would affect the stability or the length of the time that the ice is on Hudson Bay or the Arctic waters, is going to have immediate impact on polar bears." To state the issues simply and clearly: polar bears need ice, and global warming may be taking it away from them.

Identify Cause and Effect

Circle the cause and underline the effect in each of the sentences.

1. One way that the polar bear survives freezing conditions is by building up fat reserves on its body.

2. The polar bears' blubber reserves are lower because they haven't hunted in a long time.

3. The ice is melting earlier, which means that polar bears have less time to hunt seals and other food.

7. In paragraph 1 on page 11, 'He' in 'He's not in bad shape' refers to:
   A. a tundra buggy
   B. an animal
   C. Nikita Ovsyanikow
   D. a visitor

8. According to the writer, a 'top killer' is an animal that:
   A. doesn't get killed by predators
   B. kills the most prey
   C. eats umbrella species
   D. kills only predators

9. According to Ovsyanikow, when an umbrella species is threatened:
   A. The species usually evolves.
   B. Scientists are delighted.
   C. The climate begins to change.
   D. Many other species are affected.

10. On page 12, the word 'desperately' implies a sense of:
   A. exhilaration
   B. bitterness
   C. hopelessness
   D. astonishment

11. Which is an appropriate heading for page 17?
   A. Decline in Hunting Days
   B. Bay Freezes One Month Early
   C. Polar Bears Migrate North
   D. Substitute for Seafood

12. What have polar bears increasingly become a symbol of?
   A. the animals of northern Manitoba
   B. the problem of global warming
   C. a species saved from extinction
   D. the Canadian Wildlife Service

HEINLE Times

CLIMATE CHANGE:
NOT ONLY A HUMAN WORRY
By Margaret Benning

New York, June 4

In the past century, the earth's temperature has risen by approximately 0.6 to 0.8 degrees Celsius. Scientists believe that this is the result of an enhanced greenhouse effect, which is the process by which the earth maintains its temperature. Recently, a rise in certain types of gases, such as carbon dioxide (CO_2), has increased the amount of heat trapped near the earth's surface by the effect. This increase has resulted in an insulating and warming of the planet. These problematic gases, or 'greenhouse gases,' come from car and truck exhaust, factory smoke, and the burning of certain substances for heat and light. If alternative methods of producing energy are not found soon, the earth's temperature will likely rise between 1.4 and 5.8 degrees Celsius by the end of the 21st century.

Extreme temperature changes, such as those projected over the next 100 years, could be a serious threat to the human environment. However, the effects of global warming will most likely appear in animal populations first. In fact, certain changes have already been observed. For example, early thaws in the ice of the Bering Sea have affected the mating season

Annual Carbon Emissions by Region Years 1800–2000

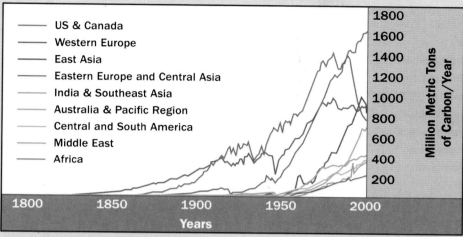

Legend:
- US & Canada
- Western Europe
- East Asia
- Eastern Europe and Central Asia
- India & Southeast Asia
- Australia & Pacific Region
- Central and South America
- Middle East
- Africa

Y-axis: Million Metric Tons of Carbon/Year (200, 400, 600, 800, 1000, 1200, 1400, 1600, 1800)

X-axis: Years (1800, 1850, 1900, 1950, 2000)

Source: Robert Rohde, Global Warming Art

of several types of seals. Certain species of birds are changing their nesting patterns as well. Certain plants are flowering earlier, and other large animals are changing their annual periods of sleeping and waking. According to Stanford University, global warming has directly resulted in biological changes to 1,473 species around the world.

Environmental groups, both governmental and private, are currently working to decrease the amount of dangerous gases, or 'emissions,' released each year. One of the first international gatherings organized by the United Nations to approach the problem produced a document which eventually became known as the 'Kyoto Protocol.'

Its aim was to stabilize greenhouse gas levels to prevent dangerous changes in the world's climate. The agreement set limits on the amounts of greenhouse gases that each participating nation could release each year. Unfortunately, the agreement didn't include strict enforcement procedures for implementing the program, and as of 2008, several countries only participate in the plan on a reporting basis. Others, including the United States, have refused to sign the document.

CD 1, Track 04

Word Count: 365
Time: _____

Vocabulary List

Arctic (2, 3, 4, 7, 11, 14, 17, 18)
bay (2, 3, 4, 7, 8, 14, 17)
beluga whale (2, 3, 12)
binoculars (8)
blubber (2, 7, 15)
carnivore (2, 4)
consequence (17)
ecosystem (17)
food chain (11)
fur (2, 7)
global warming (3, 14, 17)
ice pack (3, 7)
inhospitable (4)
insulate (7)
marine mammal (2, 4)
onset (7)
seal (2, 3, 12, 14, 15)
species (3, 11, 18)
stranded (8)
thaw (3, 17)
thrive (4)
umbrella species (11, 17)